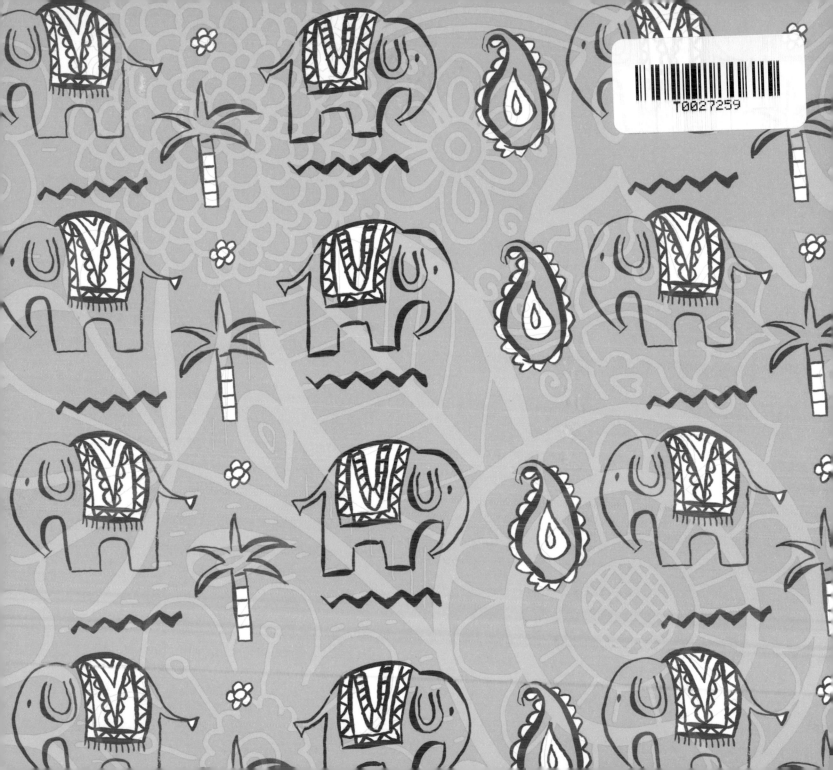

My First Book of
Hindi Words

For Naaya, with love
— Rina Singh

Dedicated to Layla and Gibran
whose stories I love to hear!
— Farida Zaman

My First Book of Hindi Words

An ABC Rhyming Book of Hindi Language and Indian Culture

by Rina Singh

Illustrated by Farida Zaman

TUTTLE Publishing

Tokyo | Rutland, Vermont | Singapore

Preface

My First Book of Hindi Words introduces young children to the Hindi language and Indian culture through simple words.

Hindi is the official language of India but not everyone living there speaks Hindi. That is because India is a complex country with 22 main languages and about 500 dialects. That's a lot of languages! Maybe it was confusing for the Government of India too, so in 1965, Hindi was made the official language. It may not be spoken everywhere in India but it is widely understood.

Hindi is written from left to right. It uses the Devanagari script, which has fourteen vowels and thirty-three consonants and is recognizable by the horizontal line that runs along the top of the letters. The 'x' sound does not start any word, but for this book I chose to include the word Xmas because it's celebrated with great enthusiasm in India.

Hindi is a living language and has taken words from other languages, such as *injun* (engine) which comes from English and *zukhaam* (a cold) from Urdu. Hindi and Urdu speakers understand each other but cannot read each other's scripts, unless of course they know both the languages.

When I was asked to write this book, I went on a search to find words that children in India might use every day but that also sounded fun. The word *dabba*, for example, is the lunch box that children in India carry to school every day, and all children sometimes have an *ulta-pulta*—or topsy-turvy day! I also added words like *patang*, which shows the love Indians have for kite-flying, and *chai*, the word English has adopted to describe the favorite drink of India—hot tea with milk and sugar!

I hope your children enjoy learning these Hindi words and looking at the colorful pictures made by Farida. If they happen to travel to India they can make new friends and show off the words they have learnt.

Or they can surprise people by saying *Namaste*!

Rina Singh
Toronto, Canada.

A is for *akaash*.
A **sky** so blue
where little birds fly
and big planes, too.

आकाश
Akaash

5

भाई

Bhai

B is for *bhai*.
Yes, that's my **brother**.
We fight just a little
but love each other.

6

चाय

Chai

C is for **chai**.
A hot cup of **tea**—
with milk and sugar,
made just for me.

7

डब्बा Dabba

D is for **dabba**.
A **box** filled with lunch—
rice and curry
and carrots to munch.

8

एक और
Ek Aur

E is for *ek aur*.
"One more! One more!"
I pester my mom
when we go to the store.

9

फ़िरनी

Firni

F is for *firni*.
It's finger-licking good!
I'd eat **rice pudding**
all day, if I could.

10

गुब्बारा

Gubbara

G is for *gubbara*.
My daring **balloon**.
Let go! And it goes
all the way to the moon.

हाथी
Haathi

H is for *haathi*.
What a fun ride!
The **elephant** sways me
from side to side.

12

इन्जन
Injun

I is for *injun*.
The **engine** roars!
The train is leaving—
please close the doors.

13

झूला

Jhoola

J is for ***jhoola***.

The **swing** goes high,
higher and higher—
till I touch the sky!

14

कहानी

Kahani

K is for *kahani*.
My grandma tells
a **story** of magic,
adventure
and spells.

लट्टू
Lattoo

L is for **lattoo**.
Spin! Spin! Roll!
My **spinning top**
is out of control.

16

मोर

Mor

M is for **mor**.
We all love the way
the **peacock** fans his feathers
in brilliant display.

नमस्ते
Namaste

N is for *Namaste*.
We join our hands for **greeting**
uncles, aunts, cousins—
Whoever we're meeting.

ओले

Olay

O is for **olay**.
Hide under our beds!
Hailstones are falling
and hurting our heads!

19

पतंग
Patang

P is for **patang**.
Flying so high!
I watch from the rooftop,
my **kite** sails the sky.

20

क़दम
Qadam

Q is for **qadam**.

Each **step** has a sound.
My sister tiptoes softly,
I stomp on the ground.

21

रंग Rang

R is for **rang**.
*Holi, the festival of **colors** is here!*
Red, yellow, blue
flying everywhere!

22

सडक
Sarak

S is for **sarak**.
The **road**—crazy busy!
Cars, cows and people!
No wonder we're dizzy.

23

ताऱा

Tara

T is for **tara**.
A **star** shining bright—
twinkle twinkle
all through the night.

24

उल्टा पुल्टा
Ulta-pulta

U is for **ulta-pulta**.
What can I say—
It's all upside-down
on a **topsy-turvy** day.

वृक्ष
Vriksh

V is for **vriksh**.
Let's go shake the **tree**.
I'll catch the mangoes—
one, two, three.

26

वाह
Wah

W

is for **wah**.
Oh, **WOW!** Say my aunts when I show them how beautifully I can dance.

कष्ट तरंग
Xylophone

There is no X in the Hindi language, but India has lots of musical instruments. The Kasht Tarang is a special kind of xylophone because the wood makes a very beautiful sound.

is for **Xylophone**
It sounds really good.
Kasht Tarang we call it.
It is made out of wood.

28

यात्रा

Yatra

Y is for **yatra**— a **journey** that brings new places and faces and many new things.

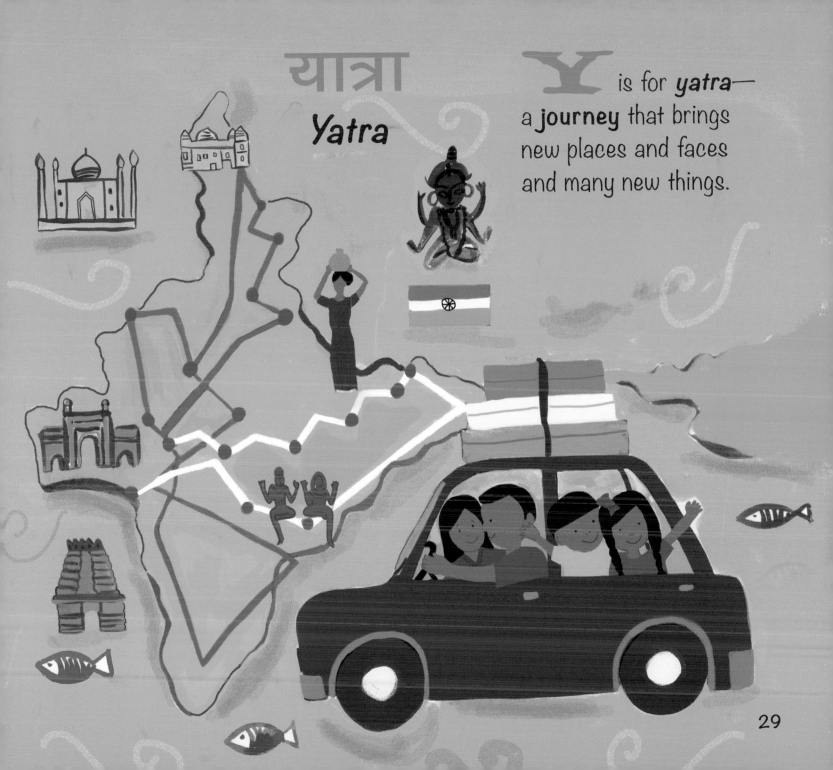

जुखाम
Zukhaam

र

is for **zukhaam**.
Achoo! I sneeze.
I've got **a cold**!
Mama, hug me please.

30

List of Words

Akaash   Sky

Bhai   Brother

Chai   Tea

Dabba   Box

Ekaur   One more!

Firni   Rice pudding

Gubbara   Balloon

Haathi   Elephant

Injun   Engine

Jhoola   Swing

Kahani   Story

Lattoo   Spinning top

Mor   Peacock

Namaste   Greeting

Olay   Hailstones

Patang   Kite

Qadam   Step

Rang   Colors

Sarak   Road

Tara   Star

Ulta-pulta   Topsy-turvy

Vriksh   Tree

Wah   Wow!

Xylophone (Kasht Tarang)

Yatra   Journey

Zukhaam   A Cold

Published by Tuttle Publishing, an imprint of Periplus Editions (HK) Ltd.

www.tuttlepublishing.com

Library of Congress Control Number: 2015957086

ISBN 978-0-8048-5013-1
(Originally published with ISBN 978-0-8048-4562-5)

Distributed by

North America, Latin America & Europe
Tuttle Publishing, 364 Innovation Drive
North Clarendon, VT 05759-9436 U.S.A.
Tel: 1 (802) 773-8930
Fax: 1 (802) 773-6993
info@tuttlepublishing.com
www.tuttlepublishing.com

Japan
Tuttle Publishing, Yaekari Building, 3rd Floor,
5-4-12 Osaki, Shinagawa-ku, Tokyo 141 0032
Tel: (81) 3 5437-0171
Fax: (81) 3 5437-0755
sales@tuttle.co.jp
www.tuttle.co.jp

Asia Pacific
Berkeley Books Pte. Ltd., 3 Kallang Sector #04-01,
Singapore 349278
Tel: (65) 6741-2178
Fax: (65) 6741-2179
inquiries@periplus.com.sg
www.tuttlepublishing.com

Indonesia
PT Java Books Indonesia, Kawasan Industri Pulogadung
JI. Rawa Gelam IV No. 9, Jakarta 13930
Tel: (62) 21 4682-1088
Fax: (62) 21 461-0206
crm@periplus.co.id
www.periplus.com

25 24 23 22 21
10 9 8 7 6 5 4 3 2 1

Printed in Malaysia   2104TO

"Books to Span the East and West"

Tuttle Publishing was founded in 1832 in the small New England town of Rutland, Vermont [USA]. Our core values remain as strong today as they were then—to publish best-in-class books which bring people together one page at a time. In 1948, we established a publishing office in Japan—and Tuttle is now a leader in publishing English-language books about the arts, languages and cultures of Asia. The world has become a much smaller place today and Asia's economic and cultural influence has grown. Yet the need for meaningful dialogue and information about this diverse region has never been greater. Over the past seven decades, Tuttle has published thousands of books on subjects ranging from martial arts and paper crafts to language learning and literature—and our talented authors, illustrators, designers and photographers have won many prestigious awards. We welcome you to explore the wealth of information available on Asia at **www.tuttlepublishing.com**.

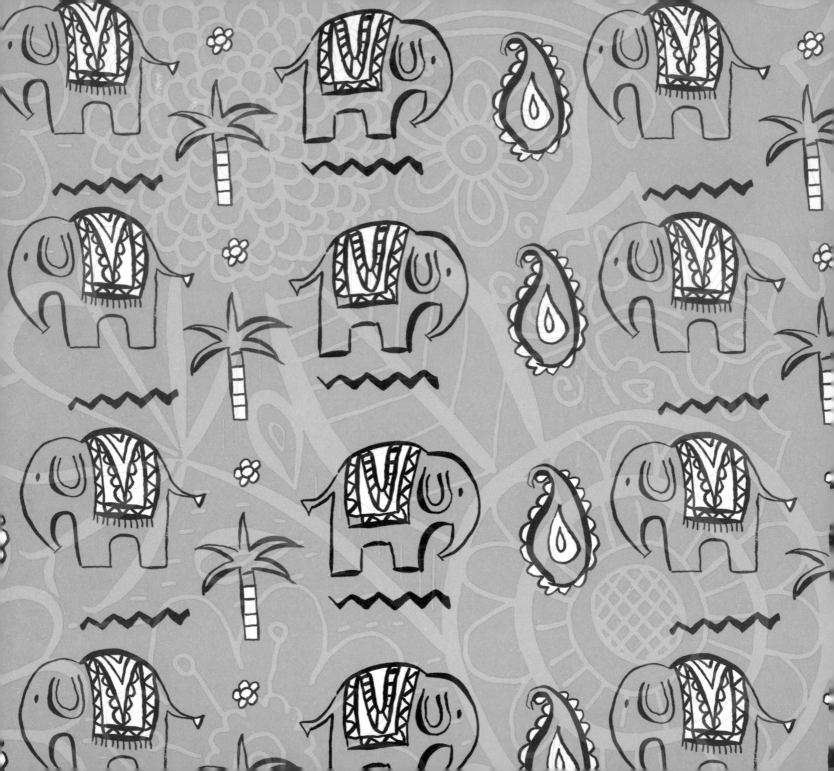